D0627524

bush
PUBLISHING
& associates

# Testimonies

*Mom's call, telling my wife Sue and me that Ruth Ann had landed safely in Los Angeles with Katie and Art in her custody, surprised us. Of necessity, the rescue plan had to be secret and tightly guarded against all but those who played a role in carrying it out. Once Mom finished describing the extraordinary events of the three days just passed, the tension of all the preceding months – the disbelief, the fear, the anger, the grief of losing Katie and Art – suddenly gave way to a flood of relief and joy. So few stories of disappearing children end so happily.*
– Roger, brother

*The memory that stays with me is from early one summer when I stopped by Ruth Ann's home for a visit: I was shown to the room where I was to stay. Being a schoolteacher, I naturally scanned my environment. My eyes rested on a stack of unopened Christmas gifts. Ruth Ann told me they were waiting for Katie and Art. Just the memory brings tears – I felt the reality of the loss, the emptiness of the lack of "kid sounds." There are no words to express the hollowness I felt to the core. Up until that point, it had been merely an intellectual experience for me. Another level of memory surrounding this visit was how Ruth Ann used the Bible as a source of strength and understanding. I remember feeling a calm for her because she had this support.*
– Judy, friend

*After the children were located and returned [to the United States], all mail [to and from Ruth Ann's family] was routed through me to avoid tracing them to their new home. Calls, presents, and messages were handled with caution. I did get a few phone calls, and I remember being so concerned that I do not reveal where the family was. I was determined to not to let information get out – it had taken, it seemed, nearly a year to get the children back.*
– Rae Marie, sister

*Being kidnapped at the age of seven, even by a parent, is a traumatizing experience that can color every aspect of your life from that point forward. This is a story of what happened to my brother and me and how my mother's faith and perseverance enabled her to finally bring us home.*
– Katie, daughter

*What I remember as a five-year-old going to see my dad around Christmas time . . . We drove to see my grandparents in Colorado, and after that, we were supposed to go back home, . . . but we didn't. Dad asked if we wanted to go on a plane. We drove to Salt Lake City, Utah, and the car was stolen. The next thing I knew we were in Australia. We stopped in Hawaii on the way. I remember not being able to be with my mom, and I missed her a lot. I knew something was wrong about us not going back because it was a lot longer than it was supposed to be.*
– Art, son

# Rescue

"You Have Turned my weeping...
into Dancing..." Psalm 30:11

## Ruth Ann Robbins

bush
PUBLISHING
& associates

# Copyright

Unless otherwise indicated, all Scripture quotations are taken from the *Amplified Version* of the Bible, Zondervan Publishing House copyright © 2004.

All Scripture quotations marked KJV are taken from the *King James Version* of the Bible.

# Dedication

To Katie and Art, my children, who lived through this experience: You were only seven and five years old at the time, too young to remember all the details of your "rescue." Because I want you to know how very much God loves you and what amazing things He performed on your behalf, I share this account. May it be a Stone of Remembrance for you, that in the future you may believe Him for even greater things for you and your children.

*"I will open my mouth in parables, I will utter hidden things, things from of old – What we have heard and known . . .We will not hide them from their children; We will tell the next generation the praiseworthy deeds of the Lord, His power, and the wonders He has done."*

Psalm 78:2-4

*"Fear not for I am with you; I will bring up your offspring from the east where they are dispersed, and gather you from the west; I will say to the north, give up, and to the south, keep not back; bring My sons from afar and My daughters from the ends of the earth."*

Isaiah 43:5-6

# Acknowledgment

Special thanks to Roger Phillips, my brother, who spent endless hours editing this second edition of my book. In doing so, he has made it flow so much more easily for any reader choosing to embark upon this amazing sequence of events orchestrated by God.

# Forward

We are living at a time in history when hearing about a missing child is an all too common occurrence. However, when we learn it is our own child who is missing, it is far worse.

It is for those people, especially, that I share my own, personal experience, seeking to bring encouragement and hope. God worked such a miracle for me that it still boggles my mind and causes me to feel boundless gratitude and awe every time I recount the story.

The miracle took a period of nine months to transpire. No, I did not give birth to another child, but the waiting period endured was somewhat akin to expecting and giving birth to my children all over again. The anticipation, labor pains and delivery were all analogous to that experience.

As you read this account of my own greatest personal crisis, I encourage you to reflect on what may be your own seemingly impossible situation. May God fill your heart with faith to cntrust it to Him.

Ruth Ann Robbins

# Introduction

L ittle did I know what I was being prepared for in advance. A few months before my children were taken, two significant events occurred.

The first event was a seminar, which took place at my church, taught by a visiting speaker, Dr. Roy Hicks, Sr. The lessons centered around his book, *What You Say Is What You Get*. The essence of his teaching was about the words we speak and the creative power that is in them to produce life or death. He pointed out how important our words are and how imperative it is that they line up with what God says in His Word, the Bible. Dr. Hicks also taught that just as God spoke the worlds into existence, we, being made in his image, also have creative power in the words we speak.

Because of the revelation I received in that seminar, from then on I became very conscious of everything I said and began making an intentional effort to create life, not death, with my words.

The second event of significance was shortly before my children were taken. I was going through a real soul-searching time and wanted faith to become more simple and childlike in trusting God.

As a young Christian attending college, I was encouraged to dissect, analyze and reason about everything. I had always appreciated being taught to stretch my mind in that way, but as a result, I also found myself approaching everything, even spiritual matters, in the same manner. My mind often stood in the way of just accepting some things purely on simple faith. I needed to be set free to just believe without having to always reason and understand everything. As a result, I requested special prayer to break free from the limitations of my own mind and reasoning power. Without going into all the details, suffice it to say that after three days of fasting and prayer, the Lord set me free to just believe Him with simple faith.

These were the two events that I believe helped prepare me for what was soon to follow.

# Table of Contents

# CHAPTER 1

# My Children are Missing

I t was December 1975. It all began when my current husband and I decided with great apprehension to let the children, Katie and Art, who were then seven and five, respectively, visit their natural father over Christmas vacation. On the day that the children were to return from that vacation, I went to pick them up at the agreed-upon meeting place.

They never appeared.

A few days later I received a phone call from their father. He told me they were having trouble getting back to Montana. After that call, I pictured them stuck in a snowbank, for there was a snowstorm occurring at the time along the border of Montana and Colorado. I later realized that my ex-husband, the children's father, had placed that phone call to buy more time for his real plan.

It was four or five days after the time the children were to have originally returned when we received a call from their father's attorney. The attorney told us that he himself had recently received a call from their father asking him how far he could go before the authorities would catch up with him. As the attorney described the conversation to us, he, the attorney, told the children's father that what he was doing was wrong, whereupon, the children's father abruptly ended the conversation.

The county attorney's office was informed, and an all points bulletin (APB) was issued on the children and their father. It focused mainly on the Colorado and Montana border area.

The next Sunday in church, people were given a chance to share. After a brief silence, the assistant pastor looked straight at me and asked if I had something to share. I asked him how he knew.

Prior to that Sunday, I had started reading through the Bible again by reading three chapters in the Old Testament and one chapter in the New Testament every day. During the week prior to this service, I had read Genesis 21. It was perfect timing because my concern that week was my children's welfare. Not only was I concerned about them traveling through a snowstorm, but I was concerned how some close friends and relatives responded to our situation with negative predictions of the outcome. They said things like You will never see the children again until they are eighteen years old.

Before sharing during that church service from Genesis 21:14-19, I explained how the children had not been returned to us at the agreed-upon time. Then I read:

*"So Abraham rose early in the morning and took bread and a bottle of water and gave it to Hagar, putting it on her shoulder, and sent her and the youth away. And she wandered on aimlessly, and lost her way in the wilderness of Beer-sheba. When the water in the bottle was all gone, Hagar caused the youth to lie down under one of the shrubs. Then she went, and sat down opposite him a good way off, about a bowshot; for she said, let me not see the death of the lad. And as she*

2

*sat down opposite him, he lifted up his voice and wept
and she raised her voice and wept. And God heard
the voice of the youth and the Angel of God called
to Hagar out of the Heaven, and said to her, 'What
troubles you, Hagar? Fear not, for God has heard the
voice of the youth where he is. Arise, raise up the youth
and support him with your hand; for I intend to make
of him a great nation.' Then God opened her eyes and
she saw a well of water and she went and filled the
empty bottle with water and caused the youth to drink."*

As I read that passage, I was assured by God that He knew exactly where my children were and what was happening to them. He would hear their cry and had a purpose for them. I was reminded that they were really His creation and mine only in the sense that He had entrusted them to my care. This gave me great peace, particularly when He said, *"Fear not, for God has heard the voice of the youth where he is."* God had put a real peace and joy in my heart. I knew that being in His hands, my children were in the best of hands. God was protecting my emotions as if I was being kept in a big shielded bubble.

As I shared this with the congregation, the Lord had spoken a word of knowledge to one of the women there. After the service, that woman, whose name was Marvel, came up to me and told me what the Lord had pressed upon her heart. She said she had intended to speak out as soon as I finished sharing, but because the pastor went right into his sermon, she didn't want to interrupt him. The verses she was impressed to share with me were Isaiah 44:2-5, Isaiah 43:1-7 and Isaiah 59:19-60:5. She had written the references on a piece of paper.

3

When I got home, I looked them up. Even though I knew these passages in their original context were promises given for Israel, I personally claimed them for myself as well. When I first read them, I thought maybe Marvel knew what was in the passages and purposely picked them out for me, knowing my situation. However, when I talked with her about it several weeks later, she said she did not even fully know what was in those passages of scripture, except the crucial words: *"Fear not."* On the day I first read them I told the Lord that if those verses were really from Him to me, then I needed a confirmation since what was in them was so astounding and almost too good to be true:

> *"Thus says the Lord who made you: Fear not . . . For I will pour My Spirit upon your offspring, and my floods upon dry ground. I will pour water upon him who is thirsty, and floods upon your descendants. And they shall spring up among the grass, as willows or poplars by the watercourses. One shall say, I am the Lord's and another shall call himself by the NAME OF Jacob, and another will write [even brand or tattoo upon his hand], I am the Lord's and surname himself by the honorable name of Israel."*

This passage assured me of my children's final outcome. They were, after all, my descendants.

I thumbed back to Isaiah 43: 1-7:

> *"But now . . . thus says the Lord who created you . . ., Fear not, for I have redeemed you – ransomed you by paying a price instead of leaving you captives: I have called you by your name, you are Mine. When you pass*

4

*through the waters I will be with you, and through the rivers they shall not overwhelm you; when you walk through the fire, you shall not be burned or scorched, nor shall the flame kindle upon you. For I am the Lord your God, your Savior . . . Fear not, for I am with you. I will bring your offspring from the east [where they are dispersed], and from the west; I will say to the north, give up, and to the south, keep not back; bring my sons from afar and my daughters from the uttermost parts of the earth, Even everyone who is called by My name, whom I have created for My glory, whom I have formed, who I made."*

My mind argued against what I read, and I was trying to convince myself that God couldn't really mean the passages literally. I was thinking that perhaps He was making some other point. I also struggled to believe that what I was reading was really for me until I read the third passage that Marvel had referenced on the piece of paper, Isaiah 59:19-60:5:

*"When the enemy shall come in like a flood, the Spirit of the Lord will lift up a standard against him and put him to flight – for He will come like a rushing stream which the breath of the Lord drives . . . Lift up your eyes round about you and see! They all gather themselves together, they come to you. Your sons shall come from afar, and your daughters shall be carried and nursed in the arms. Then you shall see and be radiant and your heart shall thrill and tremble with joy [at the glorious deliverance], and be enlarged."*

This last passage, especially following on the heels of the other two, absolutely overwhelmed me. I prayed, saying, "All right, Lord. I really need a confirmation that this is from You, and not just from Marvel."

I prayed that prayer on Sunday. In the very early hours the following Tuesday morning, I was on my knees crying and praying to the Lord in the spirit, since I did not know what to pray, as we are told in Romans 8:26-27:

> *"So too the Holy Spirit comes to our aid and bears us*
> *up in our weakness: for we do not know what prayer*
> *to offer nor how to offer it worthily as we ought, but*
> *the Spirit Himself goes to meet our supplication and*
> *pleads in our behalf with unspeakable yearnings*
> *and groanings too deep for utterance. And He who*
> *searches the hearts of men knows what is in the mind*
> *of the Holy Spirit – what His intent is – because the*
> *Spirit intercedes and pleads (before God) in behalf of*
> *the saints according to and in harmony with God's will."*

So at that moment, I was crying out to God about my children and believing His Spirit was interceding for me according to His will. While I was praying, part of a verse of scripture went through my mind – three times, in fact! I wanted to brush those thoughts from my mind as I was praying. Then it dawned on me that these were not just stray thoughts going through my mind, but that God was bringing that scripture to my attention:

> *"Rachel weeping for her children . . ."* That was all.
> *"Rachel weeping for her children . . ."*

I used my concordance – an index to find people, places and words in the Bible – to locate the story. I found those words in Jeremiah 31:15.

Along with more of its context (Jeremiah 31:15-17),

*"Thus says the Lord; A voice is heard in Ramah, lamentation and bitter weeping; Rachel is weeping for her children; she refuses to be comforted for her children for they are not. Thus says the Lord: Refrain your voice from weeping, and your eyes from tears, for your work shall be rewarded, says the Lord; and [your children] shall return from the enemy's land. And there is hope in your future, says the Lord; your children shall come again to their own country."*

Of course, at that point, I had no idea that my children were even out of the country!

Wow! What a confirmation that was! I had just received the third passage of scripture and assurance from God that my children would return. I just did not know how or when. The Lord wanted me to trust Him and rest in knowing that He would bring the things I had read to pass.

A week or so later, I received a letter from a friend in Virginia, Lora. She had learned from my relatives that my children were missing. She did not know, however, about the promises that God had given me concerning their return. Lora wrote, saying that she had not planned on writing but felt impressed of the Lord to write and include the following passage, Isaiah 49:21-23:

*"The Sovereign Lord says to His people, 'I will signal
to the nations and they will bring your children home.
Then you will know that I am the Lord, no one who
waits for My help will be disappointed.'"*

Up until this time in my life, I had been taught to question and
be hesitant to receive guidance from any sources other than the
Bible. This is probably why God has used His Word many times
to guide and assure me. He knew I would pay attention to and
believe His Word. *"Faith comes by hearing and hearing by the
Word of God"* (Romans 10:17). However, I believe He gave
me an extra measure of faith at this time. I absolutely knew He
was going to bring back my children. Nothing to the contrary
even fazed me. Receiving this last confirmation by way of my
friend's letter alleviated any remaining doubt that may have
lingered before.

As we continued to search and get information as to my children's
whereabouts, we faced some hindrances along the way. Due to
the Privacy Act, we could not get information from the airlines
or other transportation companies. None of them were allowed
to give out any information concerning who bought tickets or
who boarded planes, trains, or busses. Even the university in
Montana where the children's father both attended and taught
could not give us any information. After frequently calling the
police department detective assigned to work on the children's
case, he finally came right out and told me that he could make
more progress if I would just leave him alone. Although the
police department still had an APB out on them, I realized there
was nothing I could do. I felt completely helpless before God
and knew that all I could do was believe Him.

# CHAPTER 2

## Searching for Clues

About two or three weeks into January I awoke one morning thinking how the children's father could just be hiding out with them somewhere in the mountains of Montana and, perhaps, would need to go out to get groceries. If so, some little ol' lady or little ol' man might see them.

Thinking that I should have the children's photos publicized, I went that same morning to the town newspaper and asked if they would print Katie and Art's pictures. The gentleman I talked to told me he didn't think they could since there were thousands of missing children cases every year. If they did it for me, they would be expected to do the same for others. He said he would discuss it with the editor and get back in touch with me. He also said he was afraid of a legal suit, so I explained that I hoped they would at least print the children's pictures and ask if anyone had seen them.

From there I went to the local television station and asked them if they could flash pictures of the children on the television screen while asking if anyone had seen them. The gentleman I spoke with lit up and excitedly offered to shoot an interview with me and include pictures of the children. I cringed at the thought of having to be interviewed. I just did not feel up to it. But I desperately needed their pictures aired, so when he told me he would be calling back to tell me what they decided, I told him that would be fine.

Later that afternoon, I prayed that neither the newspaper nor the television station would agree to my requests unless it would help locate the children. I was concerned that later on my children would have to face their classmates from school who might have learned from the broadcast of their pictures that they had been missing.

The next morning, during my regular women's prayer and Bible study group, we agreed and prayed over the same decision.

That night I received a phone call from the television station saying that they would be over at ten o'clock the next morning to take pictures of the children's photographs and interview me. The following day I received a call from the newspaper, saying they would be printing pictures of Katie and Art with a caption stating that they were missing and were believed to be with their father. The article was to appear in the Sunday edition.

That Friday evening, the television station aired the story on both the six o'clock and ten o'clock news. Two days later, after returning from church, I received a phone call. The caller identified herself and said she had received a letter from my ex-husband and that he and the children were in Sydney, Australia. I thought surely this had to be a prank call and said, "This is not a joke!" I was in no mood to be toyed with. I was a bit rude, but she understood that I was upset and explained calmly how she had received the letter from the children's father postmarked in Sydney. The letter said they had flown by way of Hawaii. She told me that she planned to take the letter to the county attorney the next day.

I asked her to read the letter to me. She did. It certainly sounded like the way the children's father would express himself. I asked if I could at least see the letter. She agreed, so I went to her house, being skeptical and suspicious, thinking that perhaps this could be some kind of a set-up to throw me off the course of my search, for she had, after all, been an associate of his. The letter could have been sent to the United States to a friend in Australia who could then have dropped it in the mail, receiving a Sydney postmark. It could be a decoy scheme, causing me to call off the APB in the United States.

After the county attorney's office received the letter, I was told it should not be too hard to confirm his presence in Sydney since anyone who is not a natural resident must regularly report their presence and whereabouts to the authorities there.

God's timing concerning the children's photos being publicized was perfect. If I had gone to the newspaper sooner, the letter would not have been received yet, and the newspaper picture and caption would not have caught the attention of the woman who saw them. The woman who saw the picture worked in a university office right next to the woman to whom my ex-husband had sent the letter. That same woman had also seen the television interview. She then called her office colleague and asked her if the man from whom she had received the letter from Sydney was the same person she heard about on television and read about in the newspaper. Also, it just so happened that the following week the girl who told the receiver of the letter about the broadcast and news article was changing jobs and would no longer be working with her. What perfect timing that the Lord impressed me to go to the newspaper and television station when I did!

Prior to receiving information from the letter, I had regularly met with a group of people for prayer. These were people who I believed were operating in faith and the gifts of the Spirit. I believed that God would give one of them a word of knowledge concerning where the children were. We prayed concerning how to locate them, but no words of knowledge came forth. However, looking back on it later and recalling the phone call I received, I realized that God answered those prayers concerning the children's location in a more tangible way. God knew the county attorney's office would need something concrete to follow. Had I told them I just received a word from the Lord, they probably would have thought I had finally "gone over the edge" – that the whole ordeal had caused me to crack.

Based on the letter, the authorities went right into action, which led them to work with our United States congressman. After several weeks, it was confirmed that the children were in Sydney, Australia. Then, following the recommendation of our congressman, I contacted a presidential aide in Washington, D.C., who checked on the children's welfare. I had been told that the best way to get the children returned was to contact an attorney in Sydney and have them extradited back to the United States.

In my letter to the presidential aide, I asked for a list of attorneys in Sydney. Once I received the list, I selected one I believe God directed me to retain as our attorney. I called him to establish us as his client, and from that point, we corresponded by mail. I sent many documents of proof that the children were legally mine and that I had legal custody.

All I could do after that was pray and wait. In the meantime, the aide in Washington checked on the children's welfare and found that they were physically provided for and that there were no signs of mistreatment. When he called to assure me of those concerns, he also made a point to let me know their exact address and the name of the school they attended.

# CHAPTER 3

## *Plodding in Slow Motion*

Somewhere within this time-frame while being seated in the county attorney's office one day, it was hinted to me that I should consider flying to Sydney, to the children's location. Up to that point, I had not even entertained the idea since I had no financial means to travel. The entire ordeal of being without my children had drained me of any courage I had before. Although my heart continually ached and whenever I would hear the sound of children playing I would get a sinking feeling, I immediately dismissed the thought of flying to Sydney.

As time passed, I stuck to my regular Bible reading – three chapters in the Old Testament and one chapter in the New Testament every day. I also prayed the best way I knew how. God kept giving me verses out of His Word that confirmed to me His protection of my children and their soon return. He kept my heart full of faith and hope, and in my spirit, I knew they were coming back.

Every now and then, someone would come up to me and give me money, stating that I would need it to get my children back. My first thought was that I would not need it because God was going to return them to me. Nevertheless, every time someone gave or sent money to me I put it into a dedicated savings account which I opened the first time I received money. I never asked for money, nor even hinted there was a need because I personally did not believe that it was going to require money to get my children back. I had believed that God was going to do a "Philip-transport-thing" and miraculously transport them back the same way he transported Philip back after he had shared with the Ethiopian eunuch (Acts 8:29-40).

In July, I received the first bill from my attorney in Sydney. It was for $500. I had not kept track of exactly how much money people had given me, but when I went to the bank to take out what was in the savings account, much to my surprise the amount was $500! Since the U.S. dollar at that time was worth less than the Australian dollar, I needed a total of $550 to make $500 in Australian money. I added $50 of my own money to the total, which at the time I saw as a seed I needed to plant toward getting my children home. The math was good. I put in $50, and God put in $500 – not a bad investment, I'd say. This was a wonderful encouragement to me, and it helped my faith to grow.

Because God chose not to do the "transporting" thing and drop the children right in the middle of my living room, my patience also grew. Just as James 1:2-4 says,

> *"Consider it wholly joyful . . . whenever you are enveloped in or encounter trials of any sort, or fall into various temptations. Be assured and understand that the trial and proving of your faith bring out endurance and steadfastness and patience. But let endurance and steadfastness and patience have full play and do a thorough work, so that you may be a people perfectly and fully developed with no defects lacking in nothing."*

By simple definition, patience takes time to develop. The way I see it all now, looking back, if I had gotten the children back immediately, there would not have been the opportunity for either faith or patience to develop. I Peter 1:6-7 reads,

*"Be exceedingly glad on this account, though now for a little while you may be distressed by trials and suffer temptations, so that the genuineness of your faith may be tested, [your faith] which is infinitely more precious than the perishable gold which is tested and purified by fire."*

Now, that's worth having – faith tested and purified, more precious than gold!

About a month or two before Katie and Art were abducted, a blessing had taken place. I had gone through a time of completely forgiving their father. I had let go of any resentment or bitterness I had toward him for anything in the past. In fact, I had gone through the same cleansing with regard to all of the significant people in my life. It left me utterly free, spiritually and emotionally. So when all of this occurred, and I realized he was not bringing them back after their Christmas visit, I was determined to stay free, and I refused to be taken captive by resentment and failure to forgive. Staying free in this way meant that the decisions I would be making would be based on a conviction of what was the right thing to do, not based on a negative reaction from hurt or anger. During this whole time, I never did get sucked into that vicious negative cycle. And because of all God's promises to me that I would get Katie and Art back, my heart was full of faith. Therefore, I did not give in to fear.

One of the thoughts that would flit through my mind quite often was wondering how Katie and Art were doing emotionally.

What were they thinking and feeling about why they weren't home with me? To keep from breaking down, I would not allow myself to dwell on those thoughts. However, being very concerned about their physical and emotional welfare, I requested the authorities to check on them. Beyond praying for them, I felt utterly helpless to reach out to comfort them. Even after the authorities in Washington, D.C. located them, their school and where they lived, I knew I did not dare write to them for fear of letting their father know that I knew where they were, making him more guarded and possibly even prompting him to move them to an untraceable location. I also assumed that even if I were to write to the children, he would never allow them to see the letters. I felt caught between a rock and a hard place. So, the only way I could handle it was to pray for them, leave them in God's hands, and not mentally or emotionally dwell on how they may have been feeling. I felt this was not an everyday game of hide-and-seek, but rather that the children's father was playing for keeps.

Emotionally, the hardest times I had were after a recurring dream in which I had the children back, only to wake up in the morning and realize it was just a dream. As soon as the reality hit that I did not have them, my heart would sink and become very heavy. That sinking feeling was the worst. There were a few times I was able to cry, but the worst time was the night just before God brought to my mind in prayer those verses from Jeremiah:

> *"Rachel is weeping for her children . . . thus says the*
> *Lord: Refrain your voice from weeping and your eyes*

*from tears . . . there is hope in your future . . . your*
*children shall come home again to their own country"*
*(Jeremiah 31:15-17).* After that, the crying stopped.
Hope took its place.

But the sinking feeling brought on by the dreams continued. It usually only lasted a short time – minutes – and it never developed into depression. Hope and depression are incompatible, I believe.

Two of my dreams were vividly significant, and I took them as dreams from the Lord. In these dreams, two common features stood out to me. First was the great difficulty it would require for me to get Katie and Art back. The second was the fact that I would get them back while they were still small children. I had these two dreams just a few nights apart.

In the first dream, I was climbing alone up a mountain – a very steep and difficult mountain. It took great effort to climb, and there were many obstacles. It took a long time to reach the top, but when I finally crossed over the peak of the mountain and was on the down side, my descent was very rapid. I had both of my children in my arms, and they were still very young.

The second dream was similar but in a completely different setting. I was alone on a bicycle pedaling up a very steep hill. It was very tiring and took me a long time. When I finally reached the top of the hill and started down the other side, the bicycle was almost out of control it was going so fast. But I noticed Katie and Art were with me, and they were still very young.

Of course, when I woke up from each of these dreams, my heart sank realizing they had only been dreams. But it was after the second dream that I felt confirmation from God that I would get my children back while they were still young. I also thought about Pharaoh's dreams, about which Joseph explained,

> *"The reason the dream was given to Pharaoh in two forms is that the matter has been firmly decided by God, and God will do it soon" (Genesis 42:32).*

I was certain that God had given me those dreams.

# CHAPTER 4

## Visiting Helena

During the following spring on a beautiful sunny day, I took a trip to Helena, Montana. Enjoying the change of scenery, I decided to do some window shopping to kill time.

I don't remember exactly how the conversation started, but I was talking with another customer at one of the stores, and she asked me if I had children. I said yes, but they were not with me at the moment; rather, they were with their father, who had taken off with them. She immediately understood the situation but did not understand my attitude. She responded with the fact that she had a friend who had the same thing happen to her, and as a result, she had a nervous breakdown six months later. After giving me that cheery bit of information, she remembered yet another person who, soon after having her children taken, developed a brain tumor and died!

My immediate response to her was, "Well, that's not going to happen to me because God has given me several promises that I'm going to get my children back. The only thing I don't know at this point is exactly when or how."

I smiled a big, genuine smile as I left her. She probably thought I had flipped out. In fact, I wouldn't be surprised if she added my story to her list of "Kidnapped Children" stories and told people about this crazy lady she met who had really cracked up, thinking God Himself was talking to her.

Another time that spring, I was sitting in church on a Sunday morning listening to a sermon on Jonah. Our pastor was telling how much God loved Jonah and how He kept pursuing him even though Jonah kept running. He also told of the consequences that Jonah suffered because of having chosen to run instead of obeying God.

As I sat there listening to the sermon, I kept picturing my own consequences, and I became very concerned. If there was anything I did not want to be doing, it was running from God or disobeying Him. I was asking myself if my children being taken was a consequence of disobedience. While sitting there, I prayed very earnestly – with my eyes wide open as the pastor continued with his sermon – "Lord, am I in some way running from You? I don't think I am, but I don't want to be if I am."

I no sooner prayed that prayer than our pastor stopped right in the middle of his sermon and looked at me and said, "Ruth, the Lord has a word for you, and it's from Jeremiah 29:11."

Needless to say, I immediately looked up the scripture as the pastor continued his sermon. I sat reading the verse:

> *"For I know the thoughts and plans that I have for you, says the Lord, thoughts and plans for welfare and peace, and not for evil, to give you hope in your final outcome."*

Reading this scripture completely put my mind at ease. God was assuring me right when I needed it. He had plans for me, and they were for my welfare, not for evil. Also, the final outcome was full of hope. Now I must say, that was the fastest answer to prayer that I had ever received! It assured me, in case I had any doubt at all, that God was right there with me, concerned and listening when I talked with Him.

My relationship with God had not always been this way – praying to Him and receiving such direct answers. In fact, my relationship with the Lord did not begin until I was eighteen years old. For the two years prior to that, I had really struggled with it. Having attended church most of my life, I knew deep down I really did not know God, yet I wanted to know Him. I had been raised to believe that the important thing was to try to be good and work my way to heaven by following Jesus's example. That view left me hoping but never knowing if I would make it. But more important to me was the awareness deep in my heart that I really did not have a relationship with God. I did not know how to go about establishing one, yet I longed for it.

During my freshman year in college, my roommate had a book entitled *Mere Christianity,* by C. S. Lewis. I read it one night while she was at the library. As I read the book, it made sense to me for the first time why Christ died on the cross.

All of a sudden I realized that trying to be good and working my way to heaven was missing the whole point of the Bible. The reason God became man, Jesus Christ, and died on the cross was to pay for all sin so that we could be made righteous with Christ's righteousness. In other words, we could be put in the right standing with God and become His children. God could then look on anyone who believed in Jesus and accepted His death on the cross for them as perfect because of Jesus's perfection, not one's own. I finally saw that it was not because of who I am, nor because of how good I was trying to be, but because of who Jesus is that God would accept me. It was Jesus's death on the cross, not my good works, that bridged the chasm between God and me.

That same night when I realized these truths, I got down on my knees – my way of telling God I was serious about what I was about to do – and I told Him I finally believed Who Jesus Christ was and finally understood why He had to die on the cross. Up until that time somehow I had always viewed Jesus's death on the cross as no big deal. After all, I could die on a cross, too. So what? I then thanked Jesus for dying for me and asked Him to take over my life completely. I told Him I wanted His will for my life, no matter what, even if it meant being an old maid missionary in Africa. I told Him to hang onto me no matter what. I asked Him to ignore me if I ever asked Him to do otherwise.

The next day, after praying this way, I noticed I had such peace with God – somehow I knew my relationship with Him was right. I began reading the book of Romans. It was the first time the Bible had really made sense to me. It was like the lights had been turned on. I had taken courses in the Bible and had read it through, but I had never before been able to understand its meaning.

My attitude toward people took a complete turn-around. Up until that time I had been very self-conscious and self-centered. But after I prayed that night and asked Jesus to come in and take over, I became genuinely concerned for other people, focusing on them and their needs. But the best of all was that I could now relate to God one-on-one. That was my introduction to God and the beginning of my prayers being heard and answered. It was the beginning of growing to know Him intimately.

# CHAPTER 5

## *Receiving the News*

A s the summer progressed, I kept waiting to hear the decision that was to be made in Canberra, Australia: Would Australia extradite my children back to me in the United States?

One morning I went to the assistant district attorney's office to find out if he had heard any news yet. I was not prepared to hear what he, Chuck, told me: Canberra would not be extraditing the children back to this country.

I sat dumbfounded. My response was something like, "I don't believe it. It's not true! I know I'm getting my children back." I walked out of his office almost numb with disbelief at the news.

Later that afternoon at home, I received a phone call from the son of Marie, a good friend of mine. She and I had been prayer partners through much of this. She had a situation in her life that she was believing God for, and I was believing God to get Katie and Art back. We agreed to pray every Monday through Friday for each other, one-half hour each day. We had been doing this for several weeks.

When her son, Justin, who was about eight years old, called, he asked if I had seen his mom. He was now home from school, and she was usually there when he arrived. I told him that I had not seen her and did not know where she was but that I would drive to his house and wait with him until she came home.

When I arrived at their house, Marie was home, having gotten there just before me. She then told me about her unusual day. Marie had gone to work at 8 a.m., as usual, but after only an hour or so, she became so upset she couldn't work, yet she had no idea why she was feeling the way she was. She asked if she could leave work and was told that would be all right.

Instead of driving home, Marie drove to a creek to be alone to pray. She climbed out onto a huge rock in the middle of the creek, lay down and cried, praying in the spirit. Marie did this all day. As she told me the story, she said she didn't even know what she was praying about.

I told her then that I knew the reason for her praying as she did: the kids and me. I told her of the news I had received earlier that morning: that the Australian government would not extradite Katie and Art. I told her how the news was so hard for me to bear that I could not even cry or pray. I also told her that as I was driving to her house, I knew that the only option I had left was to get on an airplane and fly to Sydney and physically bring them back myself. I told her that it seemed that she had been interceding on my behalf, and I believed that she had actually in prayer somehow borne the burden herself for me because I could not bear the news I had been given that morning.

I was not ever sure if it was really scriptural that she could bear my burden since it was Jesus who bore our sins, sicknesses, pains and sorrow. But the Bible does say we are to bear one another's burdens, so maybe she was doing just that.

I told her that she was not to tell anyone what I was about to do because if my children's father got wind of it, he might leave Sydney, and I'd have an even harder time locating them again. I told Marie I did not know how I would do this, but somehow God would supply me with the money and the ability to go to Sydney and literally kidnap my children back.

That was in August.

# CHAPTER 6

## *Preparing the Trip*

It took one month to prepare. By September we had sold everything we owned in a big yard sale: car, furniture, piano – everything. We got a grand total of $1000.

Without asking anybody for money and without letting anybody know what I was about to do, people sent us money. A few family members and friends were aware of my plans, but they all lived out-of-state, and I wasn't worried about word getting to my ex-husband from them. By the time we had the yard sale, the money I had deposited into the dedicated savings account for my children's return had totaled almost $3000. With the yard sale money, the total now came to nearly $4000.

It would take $3600 for plane tickets for both of the children to get to the States, including my own round-trip ticket. I purchased these stateside. With all the tickets in hand, I was left with $400 to take to Australia to pay for attorney's fees or any other unexpected expenses. It was amazing to me that God moved in people's hearts like this and that totals all came out so perfectly. I had planned none of this. All I knew was that my husband and I were willing to sell everything we had to get the children back and that God would make up the difference. He did.

The laws in the United States can sometimes work against individuals. Although the officials were doing all they could to help me get my children back, passport photos must be no more than six months old. So, when it came right down to putting the children on my passport, they would not do so because the children had been out of my possession for over nine months. Therefore, I didn't have recent enough photos of them.

The State of Montana would not back down and waive the law in my case, so I had to embark on my trip not even knowing how or if I would be able to have the children put on my passport in Australia. Was I going to have to somehow smuggle them out of the country? The whole project was at stake. Getting my children back was not a sure thing, yet it cost us everything we had. The only sure thing I knew was God's promise to me that I would have them back again while they were still young.

The night before I left for Australia, a friend of mine, Helen, had a word for me from the Lord. She felt impressed to tell me that the Lord had prepared the way before me and behind me, and that I would return from Australia with my children. As I left for the airport the following day, I told myself that I was not coming back without them, yet I was unsure as to how long it would take. If it became a messy court battle, it could take as long as three months.

On that same day, my husband, the children's stepfather, boarded a train for Virginia. He would stay at my parents' home and wait. In the meantime, he would look for a job in his field, computers, while I worked on getting Katie and Art home to us.

# CHAPTER 7

## Casing the Turf

I had called the attorney in Sydney and arranged to meet with him in the afternoon of my arrival. As we met, he introduced me to his assistant, who was a law student about to take his final bar exams in a few days. He told me that his assistant would accompany me in a taxi to the children's school in Darlinghurst. We would be able to watch for the children as school let out, and we would be able to see exactly how they went home. And so we did.

It was a rainy day, and we each used umbrellas. We stood outside the schoolyard looking through the fence, waiting for the children to make their exit. At last, children began pouring out of the doors. I anxiously watched for Katie and Art. It was easy to spot Katie, with her long, straight blonde hair. She was with a friend, and they began walking home. I could not see Art anywhere. We decided to follow Katie and her friend to see what path they would take. We would decide about Art later.

Remaining incognito was imperative, though. Back home, my friend Helen had given me some of her clothes in case I had to appear in court. I would look "more professional," she said. Even though our task today was not a court appearance, I purposely wore one of Helen's outfits on this day so that I would not be easily recognized. We also stayed a half block behind the children, and I made sure to use the umbrella to shield myself from Katie's sight in case she looked back in my direction. It was essential that their father not learn of my being in Sydney.

We followed Katie and her friend for several blocks and then took a taxi back to the attorney's office. He then sent us to meet with the American consulate.

As soon as we arrived, the consulate's first comment was, "Well, I see that you have finally decided to come. Do you have the children in your possession yet?"

I told him that we had seen Katie and a boy walking home from school, but we had not yet seen Art.

He then proceeded to tell me what I must do. He said I must go back the next day and find Art. As soon as I had them both in my possession, I was to take them to a fast passport studio, get their pictures taken, and then bring them and their photos immediately to his office. He would put them both onto my passport, and I could be on my way back to the United States.

Months prior to this, we had sent well-documented proof of my identity and proof of custody, along with other necessary papers. So, when the consulate had commented about my finally deciding to come, I judged from his experiences from similar cases he had been expecting me, even though I had not intended to come until the last month or so.

This all surprised me. Here the consulate was telling me the plan of action and willing to cooperate with me in getting my children back. I had been anticipating a possible struggle, perhaps a two- or three-month court battle. Yet here it was only my first day in Australia, and I was being given a plan that would only take a few days!

Meanwhile, we returned to the attorney's office. His assistant and I told him what had transpired. He told me I must first phone the airport and find out what options I had for flights out of Australia. The flight schedule must allow enough time for me to do several things:

- Locate and pick up Katie and Art on their way home from school;

- Have their passport pictures taken;

- Take them to the American consulate for their photos to be put on my passport;

- Ride to the airport, and finally;

- Board the plane and get off the ground before their father would have time to piece together what had happened.

But even before all that could take place, we had to locate Art and find out how he went home from school.

So we – the attorney's assistant and I – returned to Darlinghurst the next afternoon. This time it was not raining, so there were no umbrellas to hide behind. I had to be very careful not to let the children see or recognize me. We were already operating on the hypothesis that perhaps the boy that Katie was with the day before was Art, not someone else, such as a friend, although the boy was much taller and walked differently than the Art I remembered. It had only been nine months. It was hard for me to fathom this could be Art. How much can a child grow and change in just nine months?!

Again, we spotted Katie, and she was walking with the same boy. We kept a reasonable distance. It did not look like Art to me, but we knew we must find out. I lingered behind as the law student stepped up his pace and crossed the street way ahead of them so he could walk back toward them. As he approached them, he nonchalantly said, "Hi. Is your name Art?" The boy with Katie replied, "Yes." The attorney's assistant passed them and continued toward me. When he arrived, he told me that the boy said that his name was Art.

It was still a long shot, but I was willing to go with it. We took a cab back to the attorney's office and relayed to him what we were trusting was good news. He told me I must make plane reservations immediately for the next evening to fly out of Australia. He explained that I must not take a plane that would touch down in New Zealand because the children could still be removed from the flight if the authorities were directed to do so. Australia would still have jurisdiction over a plane in New Zealand, and even though I had full custody of the children in the United States, it was meaningless in Australia since Australian laws give each natural parent equal custody rights. Hence, the only route I could safely take would have to be through Hawaii as the first stop.

Unfortunately, the first scheduled flight out of Sydney was to lift off at 7 p.m. That meant there would be a few hours from the time their father would know the children were missing until the plane would leave the ground. I would have to trust God that we would lift off before any restraining orders could reach the airport.

# CHAPTER 8

## Day Three in Sydney

The morning of my third day in Sydney I woke up knowing that this was the big day I had trusted the Lord for these long nine months. I got out of bed, had some coffee and read my Bible. I was impressed to read Psalm 126. It turned out to be both a promise and a prophecy for what was about to take place:

> "When the Lord brought back the captive ones of
> Zion, we were like those who dream. Then our mouth
> was filled with laughter, and our tongue with joyful
> shouting; then they sang among the nations, 'The Lord
> has done great things for us; we are glad. Restore our
> captivity O Lord, as the streams in the South. Those
> who sow in tears shall reap with joyful shouting. He,
> who goes to and fro weeping, carrying his bag of seed,
> shall indeed come again with a shout of joy, bringing
> his sheaves with him.'"

Just as the Psalmist wrote about the rejoicing that would take place at the Lord's deliverance of the exiles, the Lord was speaking to my heart as well. He was giving me a peace and an anticipation of the great deliverance and rejoicing that was about to take place for me and my children. He had led me these past nine months by His Word, and today was no exception. These words from Him would give me the courage and faith to face what would take place this very day.

After reading and meditating on God's promise, I placed it all in His hands. I ate breakfast, went shopping for a change of clothes for the children, knowing that they would have to wear what they had on for the trip back to the United States. We would catch a flight from Honolulu to Los Angeles, and from there get tickets to Virginia, where my parents lived.

That afternoon, the arrangement that I had with the attorney's assistant was to meet with me and go for the third time to the school at dismissal time. We would also be accompanied by a Presbyterian minister whose church arranged for both my stay in the hotel and my meals while in Australia. He and his wife had both met me at the airport when I first arrived three days before. He was to drive us to the school to get my children.

The plan was that he and the attorney's assistant would stay in the car and slowly follow at a distance until I had my children. Then they were to drive up and pick us up. From there we would get the passport pictures, go to the consulate's office, go to the airport and then board the plane. They would see us safely off.

That was the plan.

But here's what actually happened. As one might expect in such a course of events, there was an unanticipated twist. From a distance, I saw Katie and the boy I hoped was Art leaving the school grounds together. Much to my dismay, however, another child and adult were with them! What to do now? Well, I followed them, keeping a safe distance, for several blocks. I was starting to become concerned because I knew it could not be too much farther to where they lived. If they arrived there, I might not be able to get them.

I waited for the pastor and attorney's assistant following me in the car to finally catch up to me, and then I hurried out to the car to ask what they thought I should do. We were all in agreement that I could not wait much longer, and I needed to get them before they got too close to home. They both thought that I would just have to explain to the woman with them that I was their mother and the children needed to come with me. We would see what happened after that.

So I stepped up my pace to catch up to them. Miraculously, just then, the woman and child kept going straight, and Katie and Art turned to the right and crossed the street! God was definitely guiding my steps. I started to walk very quickly to catch to them, and they, hearing my footsteps behind them, turned around to see who was following them. The moment I had longed for was here, but this could be a shock for them. Unlike the previous day, I had worn a dress I knew would be familiar to both of them, yet that could only go so far to bridge their possible disbelief. I said, "Are you who I think you are?"

Katie cried out, "Mommy!" and ran into my arms. Art just stood there being shy – typical for him. He still did not look like the Art that I remembered from nine months before. When I asked him who he was, he said he was Art, but he had developed a strong Australian accent, understandably. Katie had one as well. Even knowing how that would be the case, Art still did not sound like himself to me. His voice was not as deep as it had been. He was taller, too. But he still had the same light brown hair and freckles.

It was a funny feeling – kidnapping a kid off the street who looked enough like mine, who seemed to be mine, but sounded different and walked differently enough that he might *not* be mine! Art had always been quiet and shy, so it was not difficult to spot clues to his identity here and there. All of this was flooding my mind in just those few seconds.

I had not even planned what I was going to say to them. I said, "Well, you have both grown so much, I'd like to take you to get pictures taken. Shall we go?"

They agreed as I ushered them out into the street toward the waiting car. We all climbed into the back seat, and the pastor drove us off to get passport pictures taken.

As soon as their pictures were taken, we all headed to the American consulate's office. The consulate was, of course, expecting us. He immediately put their photos on my passport and told us we could be on our way. He asked me what time the plane was scheduled to leave. I told him 7 p.m. He then reached for his hat and coat and left his office with us, locking it as he left. He said, "Now, I am not going to be available for anyone to reach me until after 7 p.m. when I know your plane has left the ground." At that point, it was about 4 or 4:30 p.m. "If anybody were to ask me any questions, I would have to tell the truth that I had put the children on your passport and that you were catching a plane. If their father were to find out in time, he could then take them off the plane. But once the plane leaves the ground, you are safe."

We then went directly to the car, and the pastor and attorney's assistant drove us to the airport. On the way, I spoke with the children and at some point asked them "How would you like to come home with me for a while? It's been so long since we've seen each other."

Katie and Art both agreed they wanted to do that. I'm not sure how I would have handled it if either of them had said no. It had never crossed my mind that they might not want to come home with me.

I had always thought that when raising a child, it's best not to offer a choice if one isn't actually an option. If you are about to leave for the grocery store and there will be no one staying to watch a child, you do not ask the child if he wants to go to the store. You just say, "Come on. We get to go to the store now." Save the choices for when there really are choices, and those choices are important for the child's development in learning how to make good decisions.

So, I'll never know why I asked them. Maybe subconsciously I just wanted to know I wasn't taking them against their wills. Or perhaps I wanted to prepare them for the fact that we were about to take a long trip. The bottom line, though, was that I was already positive that we were all three flying back to the United States together. A "no" to that question did not exist.

# CHAPTER 9

## The Lure of Liftoff

We arrived at the airport at about 5 p.m., two hours before take-off. We confirmed the dates on all three tickets, went through customs, and spent the rest of the time reading books together. We also talked and ate cheese and crackers, which I had purchased earlier that morning when shopping for clothes.

Meanwhile, the pastor and attorney's assistant waited on the other side of customs. They were to call Katie and Art's father as soon as the plane lifted off the runway to tell him the children were safe with their mother. He had behaved badly and illegally in abducting the children, but it would be wrong to force him to worry that something horrible might have happened to them when they failed to come home from school. Several days later, I received a letter from the pastor informing me that he had made the call to my ex-husband the night of the flight.

At departure time, we boarded the plane. So far, all seemed okay. It was now time to take off, to leave Australia. The aircraft started to move toward the runway. I cannot even begin to describe the combination of hope and fear I was feeling at that moment. I could hardly breathe. The plane picked up speed down the runway, but I knew it was not a done deal until liftoff.

But liftoff it did. At the instant I felt the plane begin to glide smoothly into the air, I relaxed, and great tears rolled down my cheeks. Katie looked over at me and, herself playing the mommy, said, "Don't cry, Mommy. The plane isn't going to crash."

I laughed through my tears. "Oh no, Katie," I said. "THIS plane is NOT going to crash!"

Up to this time, I still had the uneasy feeling about the fact that Art did not look, sound, or walk like the Art I had known. Right after Katie had assured me of the plane's safety, Art leaned over and said, "Mommy. Let's do nose-to-nose."

That was the first real assurance I had that this boy whom I had just taken through customs and out of Sydney, Australia, was indeed my son. The kids and I used to do nose-to-nose back home all the time as an expression of affection, and this child had remembered it.

While on the plane, the Lord brought back to my mind Psalm 126, which I had read earlier that day. Because everything had happened so quickly and flowed so smoothly, and because it seemed like I was walking out plans that were not even mine, I felt I was in a dream.

> *"When the Lord brought back the captive ones from Zion, we were like those who dream. Then our mouth was filled with laughter, and our tongues with joyful shouting . . . he who goes forth weeping . . . shall indeed come again with a shout of joy, bringing his sheaves with him."*

I remembered my two dreams. The descents down were much faster than the long, slow, arduous climbs up. God's plan had taken only three days to return my children to me.

When we touched down in Honolulu at the airport, we learned that the next flight to Los Angeles was not until the next day, so we found a hotel and spent some time that afternoon walking on the beach. It was very muggy and hot – conditions I had never in my life cared for – and I remember wondering what in the world people liked about Hawaii. But, of course, I had just four days before been in Montana where it was the beginning of fall. Then I was in Sydney, where it was the beginning of spring. How could I expect my body to adjust so quickly to these unnatural changes? Not even that discomfort, though, could lessen the deeper joy in which I was bathing.

Because I was still uncertain that their father had been notified, despite the intentions of the pastor in Sydney, I was still a little paranoid about letting Katie or Art out of my sight in Honolulu. I held onto their hands everywhere we went. We had arrived in Hawaii early in the afternoon, so in addition to beach walking, we had time to window shop near the hotel. Anytime an adult came near us, especially if he might look like he might be a private detective working for the children's father, I was hyper-vigilant. I had this picture in my mind of my kids being grabbed away from me, and I was ready to fight with all my strength – a mother bear robbed of her cubs – prepared to tear the abductor apart! As it turned out, though, our way back home was never challenged. It went without a hitch. My fears were only just that, and nothing ever occurred to substantiate them. Still, I was emotionally armed. I was not losing them again!

As we walked the beach that day, I kept looking at Katie and Art and telling myself this was really happening. This was not a dream. I was overwhelmingly grateful to have them with me.

That evening, we went to the hotel restaurant for dinner and thoroughly enjoyed the company of each other. The children chattered away, telling me about their school, their classmates, their teachers, and on and on and on. We had a lot of catching up to do.

We then went up to our air-conditioned room to get ready for bed. I gave the kids their baths, and that was when I had the second confirmation. Art had an unmistakable large mole on the back of his leg. Until then, I had forgotten about it, but there it was. This was really my little boy, my son!

The next day we flew to Los Angeles. There, we slept a few hours in the chairs at the airport until the next flight to Virginia, where my parents and husband waited. I called my parents to tell them I was back in the States, in Los Angeles – *with the children!* – and to tell them we would be catching the next flight to Richmond.

Mom later told me that right after that phone call my dad took off his glasses, put his head down on his desk and cried. The tension of all those months finally found expression. I had only known Dad to cry one other time, and that was in the mid-50s when he received news that his sister, my Aunt Violet, was killed in a car crash along with her husband Milton and their young child Joylene.

Especially then, when Mom told me about Dad's response, I began to fully appreciate how profoundly concerned my parents had been about their grandchildren and me throughout the whole nine-month period leading up to that day.

# CHAPTER 10

## Virginia

Once we arrived in Virginia, I knew it was essential not to let our friends in Montana, or anywhere else, for that matter, know where we were living. I did not want my children taken again.

So we wrote letters to all our friends with my sister's New York address as the return address. We then put the letters in a large envelope and sent them to my sister who would mail them from her location. Anyone sending letters to us, then, would mail them to my sister's address. She would then repeat the scheme, putting them into another envelope, so that any letter that would be returned to its sender for any reason would go back to her, not to the original sender. This elaborate deception seemed necessary to avoid any chance of revealing our real location.

This went on for several years. If anyone were to try to locate the children or us, they would have to go through my sister, who would then notify me of the effort. I would know then to be especially watchful and cautious about the children's comings and goings. I even began volunteering at their elementary school as an aide so I could ride with them on their bus, keeping close tabs. It turned out to be a blessing in disguise because my volunteering eventually turned into a substitute teaching position both in elementary and middle school. Not only did I get to ride the bus. I was able to get paid for substituting as well. I also apprised the principal and the children's teachers of the situation, asking them never to let a stranger take them out of school.

Since our family was staying in my parents' home while looking for an apartment or house to rent, I insisted that Mom and Dad agree to never give out information about our being there in Virginia or about our staying in their house. Both of my parents were of high integrity, especially my dad. He would not lie about anything, so I knew this would be difficult for him to handle. I told them both adamantly that they were to do as I asked. It had taken too much time and energy out of me to get the kids back. They would answer to me, and I would answer to God. The blood of any distortions of the truth related to our whereabouts would be on my hands, not theirs.

I had never before talked so forcefully to my parents. They had raised me to be an obedient child, and now I was requiring them to be obedient to me. But there was no resistance. They both agreed that even lying about our location would be the right thing to do. None of us doubted the seriousness of the matter. I then let God know that I was the one He was to hold responsible, and if there was any judgment concerning lying about where we were, it was not to come down on any of my family members, but on me.

At one point during that school year, I went to bed worrying and woke up the next morning still worrying – a feeling somewhere between fear and terror – that somehow the children's father would find out where we were living and abduct them again, this time in the same way I had taken them from Sydney, Australia. But God was gracious and faithful to meet my need. That very same morning as Katie, Art and I were riding the bus to school, I still can recall the stretch of farmland we were passing. While I was sitting there, my mind gripped with worry, the Lord spoke to my heart, not aloud, but clearly:

*"O you afflicted, storm-tossed and not comforted, behold I will set your stones . . . great shall be the peace and undisturbed composure of your children."*

The Lord had brought this passage to me out of Isaiah. I recognized it and knew it was from Isaiah 50-something. My heart was immediately flooded with peace. Again, I was reminded that this was going to be a faith-walk. I was going to have to entrust my children to the Lord's hands always. Yes, they were my children, but ultimately to have peace and wisdom each day in raising them, I would need to see them as God's children.

When I arrived home that afternoon, I immediately looked up the passage. It turned out to be in Isaiah 54-11-17:

*"O you afflicted, storm-tossed and not comforted. . . great shall be the peace and composure of your children . . . you shall be far from even the thought of oppression or destruction, for you shall not fear, and from terror, for it shall not come near you."*

God had ministered peace to me way back when Katie and Art were first taken. He had worked amazing things in me and for me to get them back. Now that I had them back, He was still right there alongside me, speaking His words of comfort, peace and guidance. If there is anything I can say that I know, it is that God is a faithful God when we entrust our lives to Him.

I had never before gone through anything in my life that had built my faith in God and His Word as this experience had. I am deeply grateful to God that He had given me what must have been a gift of faith during that time. I am so grateful for the way He so totally guided me with His Word, giving me promise after promise to stand on, and keeping me in what seemed like a protective bubble.

Even now, years later, as I write this account of what happened, my experience continues to build my faith and leaves me with a sense of awe of Who God is and what He is able to do as we rely on Him and entrust our children to Him.

# Epilogue

As parents, it is never easy raising children. Making the right decisions can seem difficult at times. It is a particularly heavy responsibility to teach, train and look after our children, hoping to ensure their welfare, not only now, but as their lives unfold. Without the Lord, I don't know how some parents can make it. The only way I was able to experience peace rather than fear was to keep entrusting them to Him.

Perhaps you find yourself in the same or a similar situation, and you are desperately searching for a solution. If I were to sit down with you and share what I believe to be the main ingredients that led to a solution for me, I would make the following points to you, based purely on my own experience of God's faithfulness.

- Make sure you have a true relationship with God through Jesus Christ. Pray to God, asking Him to forgive your sins and cleanse you through the blood of His Son, Jesus Christ. Ask Jesus to be your Lord and Savior, recognizing that it is only through Him, Jesus, that you enter into a relationship with God. Understand that this is not just a religion – the ritualized practice of religious actions in a church. This is a real relationship you can have with God every minute of every day now and for the rest of your life.

- Entrust all that you are and have into His keeping. This includes your children and their welfare. Ask God to do what is best for your children.

- Don't give voice to all the negative, fearful possibilities that may happen. You have been made in God's image, and just as He created the worlds with His spoken word, so you likewise can believe. What you say will be a creative force in bringing about solutions to your most overwhelming problems. Just be sure you are believing and speaking His Word, not the words of fear, doubt and negativity.

- Read, study, fill up with and meditate on God's Word, the Bible. Meditate on what God says, not on the confusing, often negative thoughts of fear or the fear talk of others. Give voice to His Word. Speak His Word. For this actually to happen, it is important to be open daily to the Lord to speak to you by reading and meditating on His Word. His Word is your lifeline, and that is what He will use to pull you to safety. You must hang on to God's Word.

- Voice out loud to God, yourself and others the verses He impresses you with, verses whose content you believe He will bring to pass. Learn to stand on that Word, both for your own and your children's welfare.

- Continually pray for wisdom and guidance.

- Turn thought and prayer into action. Do everything you can in both the spiritual and the natural realms, leaving no stone unturned.

*"Therefore put on God's complete armor, that you may be able to resist and stand your ground in the evil day [of danger] and, having done all [the crisis demands], to stand firmly in your place." Ephesians 6:13. In other words, put on God's full armor, seeing it is a spiritual battle, but at the same time respond in every way you can to the demands of your crisis in the real world at a practical, natural level."*

- For God's Word spoken to you to have power, it is crucial that your life lines up with His Word. A life of integrity is essential; otherwise, your words will just weakly fall to the ground without accomplishing anything.

- Don't put a time limit on God, and don't put limitations on how you expect Him to bring the solutions to pass.

- Live and believe God expectantly.

*"Now the God of hope will fill you with all joy and peace in believing, that you may abound in hope through the power of the Holy Ghost."*
*Romans 15:13 (KJ)*